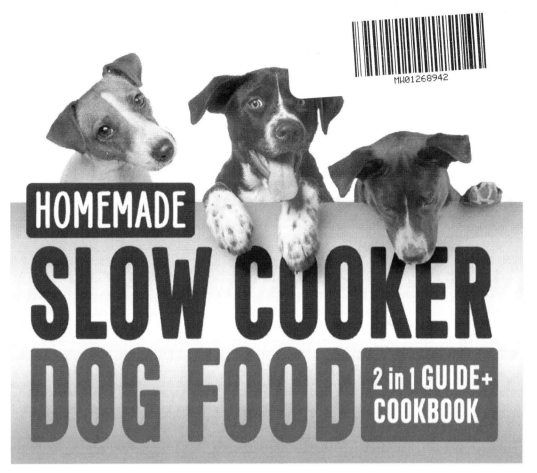

HOMEMADE
SLOW COOKER
DOG FOOD

2 in 1 GUIDE + COOKBOOK

COOKBOOK

Transform Your Dog's Diet: Discover Nutritious, Time-Saving Recipes That Ensure Health and Happiness with Every Meal, Bringing Joy to Your Furry Friend's Life.

Sophia Vance

TABLE OF CONTENTS

✦ 🦴 Table of Contents 🐕 🐕

INTRODUCTION:
WELCOME TO THE WORLD OF FOUR-LEGGED WELLNESS!

The joy you bring to your dog when you give them a bowl of food is incomparable.

As you open a can of dog food or you untie the ribbon holding the bag of kibble closed, your furry friend would already come running with wide eyes and a wagging tail. And when you finally place your pet's food in front of them, they will gobble it up in just a matter of minutes!

Unlike little children, dogs are much easier to feed.

But this doesn't mean that you should just feed them anything you get your hands on. If you want your pup to be happy and healthy, you need to focus on their nutrition. Simple as it might seem, there are many things to consider when it comes to dog nutrition.

There are many dog food products available commercially, but the problem with those is that you don't really know what they contain. This is why more and more dog parents are choosing to cook their own dog food at home to make sure that they're giving their pets all the nutrients they need.

Since you're reading this book, you may have considered this already.

You might already be thinking of the possible benefits of cooking your dog's food and how you would do it. To help you decide, here's a quick look at some reasons why making homemade dog food is a great way to go:

- It's more affordable, and it will allow you to reduce food waste at home.

- It's very easy, especially since you can use the same tools and equipment you have in your kitchen to cook your pet's food.

- It's better for your furry friend's overall wellness and health since you will be choosing all of the ingredients that will go into the food you cook.

- It's easy to store leftover dog food so that you always have something to feed your pup no matter what time of the day it is.

Once cooking dog food becomes part of your routine, you can start coming up with your own recipes based on what your dog likes. You can start with the recipes in this book and see what your canine companion prefers. Then you can go from there.

As a pet parent like you, I have found a lot of satisfaction from making my pet's food at home. When I first got my dog, I also fed him commercial dog food. Then, I became curious and did some research about those dog food products. What I found out had motivated me to start cooking my dog's food.

I have been cooking my own meals and the meals of my whole family for the longest time. Since my dog is part of my family, I figured, why shouldn't I cook his meals, too? And my pet's reaction whenever he eats his meals shows me that I made the right decision.

By the end of this book, you will understand why using your slow cooker to make your dog's food at home will make everything better. I even shared an entire chapter of recipes for you to start with.

So, if you're ready to learn the art of cooking homemade dog food, turn the page, and let's get started!

CHAPTER 1:
COOKING WITH LOVE - OVERCOMING INDUSTRIAL KIBBLE

If you go through the aisle of dog food products at any supermarket, you will see many different options. The packaging comes in different colors, and each product is adorned with its own set of promises.

But have you ever tried turning a bag or can of dog food over to read what it actually contains?

Sadly, most commercial dog food products don't contain nutritious ingredients like meat, fruits, and vegetables. Instead, they may contain various animal by-products, unnecessary fillers, and even artificial ingredients.

The strangest part is that these commercial products are so expensive!

So you need to stop buying these products and start making your pet's food at home. I promise you, this will be so much better in the long run.

DISCOVER WHY YOU SHOULD AVOID INDUSTRIAL DOG TREATS

These days, it's so easy to just buy food from supermarkets and food shops as you can find countless varieties out there. This goes for people food and pet food too. When you lead a busy life, buying food is the easy and convenient option. But it isn't always the best.

If you want to make sure that your pet is eating healthy food, then you need to do something about it. No matter how many promises are written on industrial dog treats, homemade food will always be the best. To help you understand why, let's take a look at some of the most important reasons why you should avoid industrial dog food and dog treats.

- **Most commercial dog food doesn't contain enough moisture**

  All dog owners know that kibble comes in the form of dry pellets. This makes the kibble last longer and it's easier for people to store bags of kibble at home. But in order for your dog's body to break down the kibble and get the nutrients it contains, their internal digestive system needs to rehydrate the kibble first. This could lead to your dog getting dehydrated, especially if you don't provide them with a bowl of water that they can drink out of throughout the day.

- **Most commercial dog food is highly processed**

  By nature, industrial and commercial products are highly processed. They need to undergo various processes in order for them to have a longer shelf life. Unfortunately, the processes undergone by the ingredients tend to strip off their nutrients, which means that your dog won't be getting what they need from such foods.

- **Most commercial dog food doesn't contain high-quality ingredients**

If you have ever tried checking the list of ingredients in industrial dog food products, you would probably see several ingredients that you can't even pronounce! T hen, there would be the more "common" ingredients like chicken, beef, or other protein sources. But this doesn't mean that the meat in these products is high-quality meat.

The producers of commercial dog food aim to produce food items at a low cost, which means that they won't spend a lot on high-quality ingredients. Also, it's not very common for dog food to contain "living food," such as fruits and vegetables. Your pup needs these in order to stay strong and healthy. The processing of commercial dog food also includes the use of saturated fat, which is not good for your dog's health.

- **Most commercial dog food contains unnecessary ingredients**

While commercial dog food doesn't contain enough high-quality, nutrient-dense ingredients, a lot of products out there may contain unhealthy fillers and additives that don't have any nutritional value. Even worse, some of these ingredients might have adverse effects on your dog's health when consumed consistently over time.

Even if you do find dog food products that don't contain a lot of additives, the ratio of nutrients in these isn't exactly balanced. Often, industrial dog food and dog treats may contain a lot of carbohydrates but not enough proteins. This applies both to wet and dry dog food. Protein is essential for the health of dogs, so if you aren't giving your pup enough, they can't be as healthy as they should be.

As if these downsides weren't enough, you may have already noticed how the prices of commercial dog food have skyrocketed in recent years. There are many products coming out that claim to contain ingredients that are good for your dog, but these often come with a hefty price tag. On the other hand, if you start with fresh, high-quality ingredients to make your dog's food at home, you can save a lot of money! Other benefits of making your own dog food at home include:

- You can choose which ingredients to use and how much food to make, and you can even create a menu for your dog to vary the meals that they eat every week.

- You can avoid using ingredients that have no nutritional value or the ones that your dog is either intolerant of or allergic to.

- Your dog can enjoy freshly made dog food and you can feel confident knowing that they will always be safe since the food they eat doesn't contain any unnecessary ingredients or additives.

- If your dog has any nutritional needs or health conditions, you can make adjustments to the food you're cooking for them.

Cooking food for your dog will also make you feel closer to them. Your furry friend might not be able to tell you how much they appreciate your efforts, but you will surely see the difference in their reaction whenever you give them a bowl of homemade food. While making your own dog food at home might seem intimidating, once you start, you will discover that it's actually easy, especially if you have a slow cooker in your kitchen!

SLOW COOKING: A HEALTHY AND DELICIOUS ALTERNATIVE

If you own a slow cooker, you're in luck because you can easily cook your dog's food at home. Recipes for dog food cooked using slow cookers are very simple and versatile. Now that you understand how industrial dog food products aren't the best option for your dog, you should really start learning how to cook homemade dog food.

Using a slow cooker is a wonderful way to do this.

You can buy all of the healthiest ingredients for your dog, put them together in the slow cooker, allow the appliance to do its magic, and let your furry friend enjoy the meal you have prepared.

These days, more and more people are choosing to make their pet's food at home. Whipping up tasty and nutritious dog food dishes in the slow cooker has become some sort of a trend among pet owners who want to give their best to their canine companions. Raw, whole ingredients that are combined and cooked at controlled temperatures for hours retain their nutrients, unlike commercial dog food that is highly processed.

When nutritious ingredients are cooked slowly and gently, the resulting outcome is a lot more beneficial to pets, health-wise, especially if your dog's digestive system is sensitive. As you will see in the recipe chapter, dog food dishes will contain one main protein source along with a mixture of fruits and vegetables. As these spend time stewing in a slow cooker, the nutrients they contain combine with each other, along with all the delicious flavors.

While buying dog food is easier and more convenient, if you really want what's best for your furry friend, cooking is surely the way to go. This is a much healthier alternative that you can easily fit into your daily routine no matter how busy you are. And your dog will thank you for it!

CHAPTER 2:

READY, SET, COOK!

Cooking for your canine doesn't have to be a difficult chore. In fact, it can be a fun activity, especially if you consider who you're cooking for. With a slow cooker at home, you can easily make a wide range of dishes that are both nutritious and healthy.

The great thing about a slow cooker is that you can add everything into it and then leave everything to cook for a couple of hours. cooking, you can do other things at home. When the cooking time has finished, you simply transfer the dog food to a container and allow it to cool down completely before serving. It's that simple!

TOOLS OF THE TRADE: A GUIDE TO KITCHEN UTENSILS

Cooking can be a fun activity if you have the right tools for it. Imagine trying to chop ingredients when all you have at home are dull knives. Or try to imagine how you would bake a cake if you have no measuring tools.

If you plan to cook your dog's food at home, you need to invest in the right tools and equipment. The good news is that you would need the same tools and equipment to make dog food as you would to make your own meals.

You also have the option to buy a separate set of tools and equipment for cooking dog food if you have the money to spare. Otherwise, just make sure to wash everything thoroughly after every use to ensure food safety both for you and your pet. Now, let's go through the basic items you will need for cooking:

- Slow cooker
- Bowls for mixing
- A set of knives for chopping, slicing, and dicing
- Peeler
- Cutting board
- Measuring cups and measuring spoons
- Spatulas, tongs, ladles, and spoons
- Strainer
- Skillet or saucepan
- Baking or roasting pan
- Microwavable containers
- Airtight containers with lids for storing uneaten food

You don't have to break the bank and buy all of these items at the same time if you don't have them at home. You can start with the basics like knives, bowls, an airtight containers with lids, then build your kitchen arsenal over time. As you keep cooking, you will also discover what you need.

It would be nice to keep a list in your kitchen where you would take notes or list down any items, equipment, or even ingredients that would make your cooking experience easier and more enjoyable. And whenever you have the budget for it, you can go through your list until you have everything you need!

THE MAGIC OF SLOW COOKER BOWLS: EVERYTHING YOU NEED TO KNOW

Slow cooking is a great cooking method for anyone who leads a busy life. It involves prepping the ingredients, then putting them together inside the slow cooker, and leaving the appliance to do its thing.

A slow cooker is a type of electrical appliance that makes use of moisture and heat to cook food. Unlike ovens and pans, this appliance takes a long time to cook food, but it typically results in dishes that are tender, flavorful, and healthy. Slow cookers are an excellent appliance to have at home because you can use them to cook different meals, even snacks and desserts! As it turns out, you can even cook your dog's food in a slow cooker.

Slow cookers are made of metal, and they have heating coils inside them. As soon as you turn on your slow cooker, the internal coils start warming up the contents from the sides and the bottom of the appliance. Since you will close the lid before pushing the start button, all of the heat and moisture will be trapped inside, which then allows the food to cook slowly over time.

Typically, slow cookers have a ceramic bowl where you place the food. These bowls are usually oven-safe, but they are the only part of the slow cooker that has this feature. Being quite a popular appliance, there are many slow cookers available on the market. If you don't own one yet, you can choose the model depending on your needs and preferences. Some slow cookers have basic functionalities, while others have added features. If you only plan to cook dog food in this appliance, you may opt for a simple model. But if you want to cook food for yourself, your family, and your pet in your slow cooker, you may want to look for one with added features.

In this cookbook, you will find several recipes to start with, all of which involve cooking dog food in a slow cooker. After you've tried cooking these recipes a couple of times, you may want to look for more recipes to keep your dog happy. While slow cooker dog food recipes aren't very common, you can easily find normal recipes for dog food dishes and convert them so that you can use your slow cooker. Here are a few tips for converting recipes:

- If the cooking time stated in the recipe is 15 minutes to half an hour, you can increase this to 4 to 6 hours on the low setting.

- If the cooking time stated in the recipe is half an hour to 45 minutes, you can increase this to 6 to 8 hours on the low setting.

- If the cooking time stated in the recipe is an hour up to three hours, you can increase this to 8 to 16 hours on the low setting.

You can reduce the cooking time when you choose either the medium or high setting on your slow cooker. Just remember that most ingredient combinations that include veggies and raw meat are best cooked using the low setting. This ensures that all of the ingredients are cooked thoroughly.

If you own a slow cooker, you may have already used it to cook soups, stews, pasta, and more. Cooking dog food in your slow cooker isn't that different; in fact, it's a lot simpler. To make it even easier for you, here are some tips for using your slow cooker:

- Plan your dog food menu so that you can buy and prep all of the ingredients you need.

- Prep all of the ingredients beforehand so that you can just add everything into the slow cooker when you're ready.

- Start with slow cooker recipes to get a feel of how to use your slow cooker to make food for your canine companion.

- Don't overfill your slow cooker. There should be at least a third of space in the bowl for everything to cook evenly and properly. If needed, you can cook in batches.

- Follow the settings stated in the recipe. If you would like to change the setting of your slow cooker, check the food regularly to see if it's already cooked or if you need to continue cooking.

- Be careful whenever you raise the lid of your slow cooker to mix the ingredients together or check whether the food is already cooked or not.

- After cooking, transfer the dog food to a different container and allow it to cool down completely. Don't leave the food in the bowl of the slow cooker.

It's also important to clean your slow cooker thoroughly after every use to make sure that it's ready for the next recipe you will make. Cleaning is part of a good maintenance routine, which will allow you to enjoy your appliance for years to come.

INGREDIENT SELECTION: CRAFTING NUTRIENT-PACKED DELIGHTS WITH LOVE

To ensure that your dog's diet is always interesting, you can combine different ingredients to make interesting dishes. Of course, you need to make sure that all of the components of your dog's dishes are nutritious, so that your pup can gain all the benefits of home-cooked meals.

Knowing the nutrients your dog needs will make it easier to plan their meals and the ingredients that go into those meals. You may already know your own nutrient needs, but the needs of your dog differ from ours. The bodies of dogs are built differently, which means that their nutritional needs differ too. To help you out, let's go through the essential components your dogs need.

Carbohydrates

While we get most of our energy from carbohydrates, dogs get some of their energy from this macronutrient, too. So, it's a good idea to include grains like quinoa, rice, oatmeal, and other complex carb sources in your dog's meals.

Fatty Acids and Healthy Fats

The bodies of dogs don't produce fatty acids naturally, which means that you need to supply these nutrients through the food they eat. Fatty acids and healthy fats in your dog's diet would come in the form of plant oils and animal fats. Fats and fatty acids support the structure and functions of your dog's cells, and they will keep your pet's coat and skin healthy. Adding fats to your dog's food will also enhance the taste, which will help your pet enjoy each meal more.

Fiber

Just like us, dogs need fiber to ensure the smooth functioning of their digestive systems. With enough fiber in your dog's diet, you can help them avoid gaining too much weight, which isn't good for your pet. Some good fiber sources include apples, carrots, sweet potatoes, and dark leafy greens.

Minerals

Dogs also need various minerals to keep them strong and healthy. There are many types of minerals out there, but the following are essential for canines:

- Calcium and phosphorus for strong teeth and bones. Your dog can get these minerals from cauliflower, broccoli, green beans, eggs, meat, and tofu.

- Chloride, magnesium, potassium, and sodium for cell signaling, transmission of nerve impulses, and muscle contractions. Your dog can get these minerals from whole grains, fruits, and vegetables.

- Copper for the healthy growth of bones. Your dog can get this mineral from seafood, seeds, and whole grains.

- Iodine for thyroid health. Your dog can get this mineral from seafood, dairy, and seaweed.

- Iron to support the immune system and red blood cell production. Your dog can get this mineral from poultry and red meat.

- Selenium for a healthy immune system. Your dog can get this from brown rice, vegetables, meat, and seafood.

- Sulfur for the health of your dog's nails, coat, and skin. Your dog can get this mineral from molasses, fish, and meat.

- Zinc for a healthy coat and skin and to support the immune system. Your dog can get this mineral from eggs, lamb, and liver.

As long as you make sure that your dog gets all of these minerals, they will be healthy and strong. Then you can include all the other minerals as well.

Protein

This is an essential macronutrient for dogs as their bodies aren't able to produce the essential amino acids contained in protein. This nutrient is needed to produce glucose, which would then be converted into energy for your dog's body. Lean proteins are best, but you can also give fatty cuts once in a while. Turkey and chicken are great after you remove the skin, fat, and bones; lamb and beef are good sources, too, and you can also give pork once in a while. Fish like salmon, herring, and Arctic char are good protein sources for your dog too.

Vitamins

Just like minerals, your dog needs vitamins to grow well and maintain a healthy body. You should make sure that your pet gets enough vitamins, as vitamin deficiencies could cause various health problems. However, don't go overboard, as too many vitamins can also have adverse effects on your furry friend. Some of the essential vitamins for your do include:

- choline from egg yolks, liver, meat, and fish

- vitamin A from pumpkins and carrots

- B vitamins from leafy green vegetables, liver, and whole grains

- vitamin C from fruits, vegetables, and offals

- vitamin D from fish, beef, and liver

- vitamin E from plant oils, liver, and leafy green vegetables

- vitamin K from fish and green leafy vegetables

Water

Dogs need a lot of water to stay healthy and hydrated. As you will soon discover, good dog food recipes include water, broth, or some type of liquid. Aside from this, you should also keep a bowl of fresh and clean water for your dog to drink out of whenever they need to.

Dog food recipes typically contain some type of meat as the main ingredient. You can add either cooked or raw meat to your dog food recipes. Just make sure to add this essential component, as dogs are essentially carnivores and will only thrive on a diet that's mainly protein-based. When making food for your dog, you can add the following types of meat:

- lean cuts of beef like roast, stewing meat, boneless steak, or even beef heart

- boneless and skinless poultry

- ground lamb or venison leg, butt, or stewing meat shank

If you have access to exotic meats like elk, rabbit, duck, buffalo, and the like, you can also add these to your recipes. When using fish, make sure it's cooked first because raw fish isn't good for dogs, especially when given this too often.

Next to meat, you would need to add vegetables to bulk up the dog food and increase the nutrient content. It's important to chop all of the vegetables first before adding them to your slow cooker so that they will cook evenly and combine well with the meat while cooking. Some excellent vegetables to add to your dog food recipes include cucumber, pumpkin, squash, carrots, beets, broccoli, sweet potatoes, Brussels sprouts, and cauliflower. It's also a good idea to add some fruits to the mix to add to the flavor and the nutrient content as well.

Aside from the ingredients, you also need to pay attention to the portion sizes when cooking food for your dog at home. Make sure to follow the recipes when you're cooking and serving food to your pet. It's also essential to check your dog's reaction to the food you serve as well. Do this to identify any allergies or intolerances your canine might have to certain ingredients.

Another thing to keep in mind is that there are some foods that aren't good for dogs, as these could have adverse effects on them. Some might even be toxic. Here is a quick list of foods to avoid in your recipes:

- fruits like grapes, currants, avocados, cherries, tomatoes, peaches, plums, persimmons, apricots, raisins, and the seeds of apples

- vegetables and herbs like garlic, chives, onions, rhubarb, mushrooms, and leeks

- alcohol, chocolate, nuts, cheese, cream, milk, mustard, artificial sweeteners, and salty snacks

Avoiding certain ingredients is just one step to keep in mind when cooking homemade dog food. To make sure that your canine is always safe with the food you make, here are some common mistakes to avoid:

- Feeding raw green beans to your dog. You need to cook them first to destroy certain toxins that could have adverse effects on your pet.

- Feeding raw garlic to your dog as this could irritate their mouth and parts of their digestive system. You may want to avoid garlic altogether.

- Adding too many carbohydrate sources to your dog's meals as their body cannot break down these foods as effectively as proteins.

The most important thing to focus on when planning your dog's meals and cooking their food is to balance everything well. Just like you, your pet requires a balanced diet to stay healthy. The problem with canines is that they can quickly suffer from imbalances and deficiencies, which is why you need to pay close attention. If you think that there is any issue with your dog's diet when you start feeding them homemade food, consult with your dog's vet to make sure everything is alright.

TO AVOID AND TO INCLUDE: PRACTICAL GUIDE TO SLOW COOKING FOR DOGS

Using your slow cooker to cook your dog's food isn't as different as cooking your own food in a slow cooker. Basically, you would read the recipe, follow the measurements, prepare the ingredients, and add them to the slow cooker. Press the right settings and let your appliance do its thing. Once it's done, you simply transfer the cooked food to a bowl and allow it to cool down completely before serving.

At this point, you might be wondering why you should use your slow cooker instead of all the other appliances you have in your kitchen. Maybe you're thinking about cooking your dog's food at every meal just as you would do for yourself and your family. But it's actually better to use your slow cooker for a number of reasons.

- **You can save time**

  The great thing about using slow cookers is that you can make big batches of food at a time. While the cooking time itself is quite long, you can just leave your slow cooker to cook the food while you do other things. When it's done, you can store the leftovers and simply thaw or reheat portions of your dog's food at every meal. In the long run, cooking big batches will save you time. And if you lead a busy life, this is a huge advantage!

- **You can save money**

  Buying ingredients in bulk is usually more cost effective compared to buying small quantities frequently. You can even buy ingredients for your dog and your family at the same time! Then all you have to do is prep the ingredients and throw them in the slow cooker to stew together nicely.

- **You can vary your dog's meals so they don't get bored**

  If you have enough space in your freezer, you can whip up two to three different types of dog food and then freeze it. That way, you can vary your pet's meals every day so that your pet will always feel excited whenever mealtime comes.

After deciding to start cooking for your pet, the next thing to do is to plan how to transition your pet from commercial dog food to homemade food. It's not a good idea to make an abrupt switch, as this might cause your pet to dislike the food you make. So, you need to introduce the new food gradually to help your pet adjust. Here is a sample timeline that you could follow:

- For two days, combine 20% of homemade dog food and 80% of your dog's usual food.

- For two days, combine 40% of homemade dog food and 60% of your dog's usual food.

- For two days, combine 60% of homemade dog food and 40% of your dog's usual food.

- For two days, combine 80% of homemade dog food and 20% of your dog's usual food.

After this, your next dog's meal can contain 100% homemade food. Throughout this transition, you need to keep observing your pup to make sure that they are adjusting to the new diet well. Just remember that there are no standard rules when it comes to changing your dog's diet. You just need to keep observing to make sure that you're doing the best for your pet.

If you notice that your dog is having any kind of bad reaction to the food you are cooking at home, stop for a while. Evaluate the ingredients in the recipe and go through the process of elimination. Finding out what your dog is allergic to will take time as you need to do quite a lot of trial and error. But just keep going and once you find out what's causing your dog to feel bad, you can just avoid using that ingredient.

Going back to cooking with your slow cooker, make sure to follow the recipe as it's written. In particular, pay attention to the quantities of the ingredients and the cooking times. If you plan to change the settings of your slow cooker, keep checking the contents to avoid over or under cooking your dog's food.

Making substitutions to the recipes is possible, as long as you use similar ingredients and follow the same quantities. After trying these recipes out, you may consider looking for other slow cooker dog food recipes. It's okay to do this; just make sure to search for recipes from reputable sources. That way, you won't have to worry about putting your pet in danger.

CHAPTER 3:
FOOD FOR THE HEART—ESSENTIAL NUTRITIONAL GUIDELINES

As a pet owner, you want your furry friend to stay healthy because the food you give contains all the right nutrients. Cooking homemade food allows you to choose the freshest ingredients to make delectable dishes that your dog will love.

So, how do you know that you're giving your pup everything they need?

The key here is to know what nutrients your dog needs and how much they need to stay strong and healthy. This is what you will learn in this chapter.

UNDERSTANDING THE NUTRITIONAL PROPERTIES OF INGREDIENTS

Providing the right nutrients to your pet is key to having a happy and healthy furry companion. To do this, you need to have a good understanding of the nutritional content of the ingredients that are most commonly found in dog food dishes. You have already learned which nutrients your dog needs. Now, it's time to apply what you've learned to create high-quality meals your pet will enjoy.

Familiarizing yourself with the ingredients to use is crucial so that you don't compromise your dog's health by including anything that may contain substances that are potentially harmful. Just as you would make sure that everything that goes into your food or the rest of your family's food is safe and nutritious, you need to make sure that your pet enjoys meals that will be beneficial to them.

Having this understanding will also make it easier for you to make good decisions in terms of the ingredients to use, especially when you start creating your own dog food dishes. Using the best components ensures the long-term health and well-being of your furry friend as the benefits include boosting the immune system, supporting a healthy and shiny coat, maintaining a healthy weight, and so much more.

Good nutrition comes from a balanced meal. Making sure that your pup follows a balanced and complete diet means including all of the basic and essential nutrients in every meal. This might seem like a simple task, but being able to find the right combinations takes a lot of practice, which is why following recipes is recommended when you're starting to make home-cooked food for your pet. Giving everything your dog needs will also provide them with the energy requirements they need to stay healthy. These energy requirements may vary on different factors:

- your dog's breed

- your dog's age

- your dog's growth rate

- your dog's activity level

- your dog's reproductive state (altered or intact)

- the existence of any behavioral and/or medical conditions

While keeping all of these factors in mind, you need to make sure that your dog gets everything they need from their diet so that they will have enough energy all day, every day. The proper balance of nutrients will also ensure that your dog's body will be able to break everything down and absorb all of the nutrients adequately. This is how your furry friend will meet their daily energy requirements. To help you choose the best ingredients for your canine's meals, here are some nutritional guidelines to keep in mind:

- Adult dogs need at least 18% protein from dry matter in their diet for their growth and maintenance. You may give your dog more, but don't go higher than 30%, as too much protein won't be good for your pup.

- Animal-based protein sources are the best for dogs as they contain the highest levels of the essential amino acids canines need. While plant-based protein sources are healthy, they aren't as digestible to canines because of their high fiber content.

- Adult dogs need at least 1% fat in their diet to stay healthy.

- Plant and fish oils are great sources of healthy fats. Try not to give your dog too much fat from meat.

- Adult dogs need at least 20% carbohydrates in their diet for their energy and growth.

- Complex carbs are a lot better than simple carbs. These also contain fiber, which can be beneficial to your canine.

- Adult dogs also need vitamins and minerals in their diets. There are specific vitamins and minerals to include in order to avoid any deficiencies. The good news is that fruits, vegetables, and even animal protein sources may contain vitamins and minerals. All you have to do is make sure your dog gets a variety of ingredients for each dish.

- Remember that dogs need water as well. They need to be well hydrated to maintain the proper body temperature, help break down the food they eat, provide their bodies with structure and shape, and maintain their overall health.

A good understanding of your dog's nutritional requirements and how you will provide these will go a long way toward making sure that your pup is happy, healthy, and thriving.

FEEDING YOUR DOG THE RIGHT WAY

After understanding the nutritional properties of ingredients, you will be more aware of what you're putting into your dog's home-cooked meals. But it doesn't end there. After cooking, you need to know how much to serve to your dog at every meal. No matter how nutritious your home-cooked dog food is, if you give too much or you don't give enough, your pup won't get all the benefits.

In order to keep your canine companion at the peak of their health, you want to make sure that the portions you serve are just right. Giving big portions will eventually lead to your dog becoming overweight. Giving portions that are too small might cause your pup to become undernourished or, worse, might even cause nutrient deficiencies.

Either scenario could even lead to your canine developing a host of medical conditions, such as:

- Skin irritations and disorders

- Breathing difficulties

- Congestive heart failure

- Some varieties of cancer

- Cushing's disease

And so much more. Something as simple as not giving the proper portions could potentially reduce the quality of your dog's life and even shorten their lifespan. Keeping this in mind will help you understand the importance of giving just the right amount of food at every meal.

But how much does your dog really need?

Once again, there is no standard answer to this question. The proper portion size for your pet depends on a number of factors:

- your dog's body weight

- your dog's metabolic rate

- your dog's activity levels

- type of dog food you serve

- how often you plan to feed your dog

Commercial dog food products have recommended serving sizes on their labels. Since you will be cooking your pet's food, here is a daily guide for you to use as a reference:

DOG SIZE	APPROX. WEIGHT	CUPS PER DAY	NUMBER OF CALORIES
SMALL (TOY)	3 lbs	⅓ cup	139 calories
SMALL (TOY)	6 lbs	½ cup	233 calories
SMALL	10 lbs	¾ cup	342 calories
SMALL	15 lbs	1 cup	464 calories
SMALL	20 lbs	1 ⅓ cups	576 calories
MEDIUM	30 lbs	1 ¾ cups	781 calories
MEDIUM	40 lbs	2 ¼ cups	969 calories
MEDIUM	50 lbs	2 ⅔ cups	1,145 calories
BIG	60 lbs	3 cups	1,313 calories
BIG	70 lbs	3 ½ cups	1,474 calories
BIG	80 lbs	3 ¾ cups	1,629 calories
BIG	90 lbs	4 ¼ cups	1,779 calories
BIG	100 lbs	4 ½ cups	1,926 calories

If your dog is more than 100 pounds, you can give an additional ⅓ cup for each 10 pounds. If you want to be super precise, you also have the option to use online feeding calculators such as www.pedigree.com.ph/feeding/feeding-calculator.

As you start transitioning your dog to home-cooked food, you need to observe them carefully. You want your pup to maintain a healthy weight so that they can stay healthy. You can make sure that your dog is at the right weight by looking at the following:

- Check to see if your dog's ribs are readily visible. You can't easily see the ribs of dogs that are at a healthy weight, but if you check your dog with your hands, you can feel their ribs by pressing lightly on their body.

- Stand above your dog and look down. You should see an hourglass shape where their abdominal area is narrower than their hips and chest.

- Stand next to your dog while they are also standing and look at them. You should see that your dog's chest is closer to the floor compared to their tummy.

A healthy dog looks firm without having any sagging skin or looking like they're bursting out of their coat. Make sure to check your pup every two to three weeks to make sure that there are no drastic changes happening. This is especially important when you're transitioning them from commercial dog food to home-cooked meals.

If you do see any significant change, whether your dog gains or loses weight, don't be afraid to adjust the portion sizes. Different factors affect your dog's weight and their need for specific amounts of food. So you can make adjustments as needed based on your observations. After mastering portion sizes, keep these other pointers to make sure you're feeding your pet the right way:

- As you start moving to homemade dog food, you may want to use a food scale to measure portion sizes accurately.

- If you know that your pet can be picky, start with small and frequent feedings, then gradually increase the portion sizes until you reach the recommended amounts.

- Take note of the calorie contents of the dog food that you make. The recipes in this cookbook include caloric content, but if you plan to create your own recipes, use a calorie calculator to help you out.

- Don't forget to include the occasional treats when planning your dog's menu so you can take into account the calories that the treats contain, too.

- If you notice a change in your pet's appetite, don't think it's because of their new diet right away. Other factors may affect their appetite, such as their current weight, activity levels, and age. This is why you need to observe your pet to make sure that they're adjusting well.

It's also important to keep communicating with your vet to make sure that everything is okay with your furry friend. Make sure to inform your vet of any change, no matter how small. Then, you can have a conversation about the change in your dog's diet and other tips your dog doctor might have to ensure your pet's overall health and well-being.

CONVERSION CHARTS TO GUIDE YOU

Finding the right portions for your dog may take some time and effort, but everything will be worth it when you realize that you've been helping your pup become happy and healthy. So, just keep cooking until you get the hang of making delicious and nutritious meals for your pet. To help make this process easier and more enjoyable for you, here are some conversion charts for cooking.

US Units to Metric Units

US UNITS	METRIC UNITS
⅕ TEASPOON	1 milliliter
1 TEASPOON	5 milliliters
1 TABLESPOON	15 milliliters
1 FLUID OUNCE	30 milliliters
1 CUP	237 milliliters
2 CUPS (1 PINT)	473 milliliters
4 CUPS (1 QUART)	0.95 liters
16 CUPS (1 GALLON)	3.8 liters
1 OUNCE	28 grams
1 POUND	454 grams

Wet Ingredients

OUNCES	CUPS	PINTS	QUARTS	GALLONS
8	1	½	¼	---
16	2	1	½	⅛
32	4	2	1	¼
128	16	8	4	1

Dry Ingredients

TEASPOONS	TABLESPOONS	CUPS
3	1	1/16
6	2	⅛
12	4	¼
24	8	½
36	12	¾
48	16	1

Cups to Other Measurements

CUP	OTHER MEASUREMENTS
1	240 milliliters
1	48 teaspoons
1	16 tablespoons
1	8 fluid ounces
1	½ pint
1	¼ quart
1	1/16 gallon

Oven Temperatures

CELSIUS (°C)	FAHRENHEIT (°F)
120	250
160	320
180	350
205	400
220	425

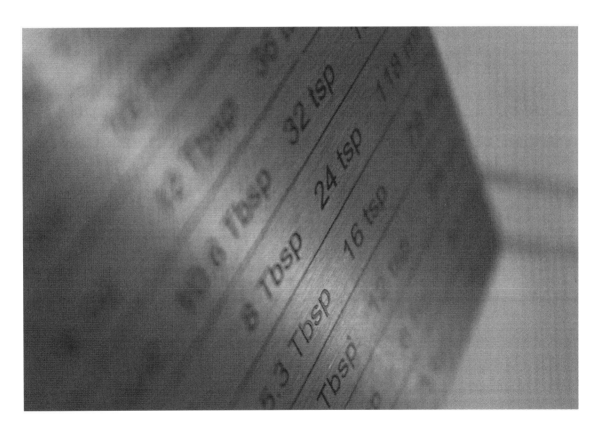

These are the basics you may need when cooking food for your dog. You can even use these conversions when following the recipes in this book. If you need any other conversions, you can easily look them up on the internet.

CHAPTER 4:
TREASURES THAT LAST

One of the best things about cooking dog food at home is being able to cook big batches in order to save time and money. But if you do this, you need to know how to store the dog food you make properly so that it doesn't get spoiled. Just as you would carefully pack and freeze the food you make for yourself and your family, you want to do the same for your dog's food after cooking big batches.

TIPS FOR STORING HOMEMADE DELIGHTS

If you have always been feeding your dog with commercial dog food products, you probably never thought about storing leftovers. These products typically contain preservatives so you don't have to store or freeze them. But freshly cooked food is different. Leaving it out for too long would end up spoiling what you made. So keep these tips in mind when storing your pet's food.

Store Dog Food in the Refrigerator

Most types of home-cooked recipes for dog food are okay to be stored in your refrigerator for up to five days. Ideally, you should divide the dog food into individual portions and then place each portion in an airtight container. If you don't have enough airtight containers, just make sure to wrap each portion tightly before placing it in the refrigerator.

Refrigerating your dog's food is essential to ensure your pet's safety. Placing portions of dog food in the refrigerator will slow down the growth of bacteria in order to keep it fresh and safe for your dog to eat, even if it isn't freshly cooked.

If you don't place your dog's food in the refrigerator, it can quickly become a breeding ground for bacteria that is harmful to your dog's health. The bacteria could cause your dog to get sick from food poisoning or even develop other types of health issues. Here are some pointers for refrigerating dog food correctly:

- Allow the dog food to cool down completely before portioning it into airtight containers and placing it in the refrigerator. If there is any lingering heat in the food, this could still become a breeding ground for harmful bacteria.

- If you seal portions of dog food in resealable bags, make sure to press out all of the air and moisture before sealing it.

- Don't overfill the bags or containers, as this could quicken the rate at which the food might get spoiled. If you are increasing the portion sizes of your pet, use bigger containers, too.

- Place the dog food containers on the bottom shelf or at the back of your refrigerator, which are the coldest areas.

Make sure the temperature of your refrigerator is always between 32 °F and 39 °F to prevent the growth of bacteria. It's also important to remember that dog food should only be stored between three to five days in the refrigerator to ensure freshness and safety. And before you serve it to your dog, smell it first before serving it to your pup.

Store Dog Food in the Freezer

If you have space in your freezer, the dog food you make can last longer when placed in this colder part of your refrigerator. Aside from extending the shelf life of your homemade dog food, freezing also preserves the nutritional value of the meals you make. You also have the option to make bigger batches of dog food or different recipes to vary your pet's meals since you can store the leftovers in the freezer. Here are some pointers for freezing dog food correctly:

- Just like when refrigerating dog food, allow it to cool down completely first before portioning and placing it in the freezer.

- Store the dog food in resealable freezer bags or airtight containers to prevent moisture from entering the food or to prevent the occurrence of freezer burn.

- Place the dog food containers in the bottom or at the back of your freezer, which are the coldest areas.

- When cooking new meals, arrange the food in the freezer depending on the date when you cooked the food.

If you keep homemade dog food in the freezer, it can stay fresh and safe to eat for up to three months. Just remember that the longer your keep dog food stored, even if it's in the freezer, the more it will lose its quality and nutritional value. So as much as possible, it's still a good idea to keep cooking and feeding your pet with homemade food instead of storing it for very long periods of time.

Choose the Right Storage

Simply keeping dog food in the refrigerator or freezer won't prevent spoilage. You need to keep each portion in the right types of containers to make sure that it stays safe and fresh. To help you out, here are some pointers for choosing the best types of containers for storing dog food:

- Airtight containers are the best option for storing dog food. They must be made of food-grade materials and they should be leak-proof too.

- Some of the best types of materials for airtight containers include glass, stainless steel, and food-grade plastic.

    - Glass containers are easy to clean and quite sturdy, but they are breakable and tend to be quite heavy.

- Stainless steel containers are also easy to clean and they're also lightweight and durable. However, they tend to be more expensive compared to containers made of glass or plastic.

- Finally, plastic containers are cheaper and lightweight, but they're not as durable as containers made of stainless steel or glass.

- Choose the right size of the containers to ensure that they can accommodate the right portion sizes of your dog's food. Remember that you shouldn't overfill the containers. If they're too big, the contents might be compromised because of the extra space.

- Another option would be resealable bags or freezer bags. You can find these in varying bag strengths and sizes. Choose reuseable bags as these are more environmentally safe.

- After using the storage containers or reusable storage bags, clean them thoroughly to ensure that they are safe and ready for the next use. Here are some steps to follow to clean the containers properly:

  - Use hot water to rinse the containers and remove all food debris.

  - Use warm water mixed with soap to wash the containers well.

  - Use hot water to rinse the soap out of the containers and remove any leftover food or soap residue.

  - Fill a basin with water and bleach, then soak the washed containers in the solution for about a minute.

  - Use hot water to rinse the soaking solution out.

  - Allow the containers to air dry thoroughly before using them again.

Choosing the right containers and cleaning them properly will allow you to feel more confident in keeping your dog's food safe and fresh each time.

Portion and Label the Food Correctly

Going back to proper portion sizes, you need to know how much food your dog needs at each meal so that you can choose the right size of container to store the food in. Then, you can plan the recipes accordingly so that you can cook just enough portions based on the number of containers you have.

Each time you cook dog food and store it in the refrigerator or freezer, make sure to label the container with the name of the recipe, the amount of dog food inside, and the date when you cooked and stored the food. Labeling the portions allows you to rotate your dog's food properly without leaving food stored for a very long time. Doing this also makes it easier for you to transition your dog into eating more food as they grow older, as you would simply have to read the labels and serve.

What to Do After and Other Tips

Following all of these storage, portioning, and labeling tips will allow you to feed your pup properly and store their leftovers safely, too. Here are some additional pointers for you to handle your dog's homemade food:

- If you let other people take care of your dog often, it's a good idea to include feeding instructions on the labels of the stored food.

- Make sure to thaw your dog's food before serving it. For food stored in the refrigerator, you can warm it up in the microwave. For food stored in the freezer, thaw it in the refrigerator first before warming it up in the microwave. Just make sure to mix the food around and check the temperature before serving it to your dog.

- Don't store any leftover dog food that has already been stored in the refrigerator or freezer. Thawed and reheated home-cooked dog food spoils easily, so you better not risk it.

Finally, before serving each portion to your dog, make sure to smell it first. If it looks or smells off, throw it out right away. It might seem like a waste of food, but feeding your dog spoiled food could cause a lot of problems, and it's just not worth the risk!

CHAPTER 5:

MAGICAL RECIPES FOR YOUR FURRY FRIEND

Making special dishes for your dog will surely show how much you love and cherish them. While cooking for furry friends is a bit different from cooking for people, having recipes to follow will make the task a lot easier! Here are some healthy and tasty recipes for you to start with.

🐕 TURKEY, RICE, AND VEGGIES

Making food for your fur baby doesn't have to be challenging when you have recipes to show you the way. There are different combinations to work with, and here is one of the more popular ones for you to start with.

Time: *4 hours, 15 minutes*	**Nutritional Facts:**
Serving Size: *7 servings*	**Calories:** *103kcal* - **Carbs:** *12.7g*
Prep Time: *15 minutes*	**Fat:** *2.7g* - **Protein:** *7.4g*
Cook Time: *4 hours*	

Ingredients:

- 1/2 cup of spinach (frozen, thawed)
- 2/3 cup of sweet potatoes (frozen, thawed)
- 3/4 cup of brown rice (uncooked)
- 3/4 cup of mixed peas and carrots (frozen, thawed)
- 2 cups water
- 1 1/2 lb ground turkey (15% fat, 85% lean)

Directions:

1. Add the ground turkey to the slow cooker, then use a spatula to break up the large chunks.

2. Add the rest of the ingredients and mix everything well.

3. Place the lid on the slow cooker and choose the high setting. Cook for about 4 hours while stirring occasionally.

4. After cooking, transfer the dog food to a container and allow it to cool down completely before serving.

5. Store the leftovers in an airtight container, then place in the refrigerator or freezer.

CHICKEN AND BEANS

Chicken is another popular ingredient for dog food because of its taste and high protein content. It's also a lot safer to cook chicken without the bones, especially if your furry friend is small and delicate.

Time: *4 hours, 5 minutes* **Serving Size:** *7 servings* **Prep Time:** *5 minutes* **Cook Time:** *4 hours*	**Nutritional Facts:** **Calories:** *297kcal* - **Carbs:** *24g* **Fat:** *8g* - **Protein:** *20g*

Ingredients:

- 1/2 cup of butternut squash (frozen, thawed)
- 1/2 cup of green beans
- 3/4 cup of kidney beans (canned, drained)
- 2 cups of water
- 1/2 cup carrots (peeled, sliced)
- 1/2 cup of peas (fresh)
- 3/4 cup of white rice (uncooked)
- 1 1/2 lb ground chicken (lean)

Directions:

1. Add all of the ingredients to the slow cooker, then use a spatula to mix everything together while breaking up the ground chicken in the process.

2. Place the lid on the slow cooker and choose the high setting. Cook for about 4 hours while stirring occasionally.

3. After cooking, transfer the dog food to a container and allow it to cool down completely before serving.

4. Store the leftovers in an airtight container, then place in the refrigerator or freezer.

🐕 BEEF AND MORE

Meat is an important aspect of any dog food dish. Here is a recipe that uses beef, is easy to make, and you can freeze all the leftovers so that you always have something ready to feed your furry friend!

Time: *6 hours, 10 minutes*	**Nutritional Facts:**
Serving Size: *6 servings*	**Calories:** *137kcal* - **Carbs:** *20g*
Prep Time: *10 minutes*	**Fat:** *1.8g* - **Protein:** *10.2g*
Cook Time: *6 hours*	

Ingredients:

- 1/4 cup of peas (canned or frozen)
- 3/4 cup of butternut squash (peeled, chopped)
- 1 cup of kidney beans (canned, drained, rinsed)
- 3/4 cup of brown rice (uncooked)
- 3/4 cup of carrots (peeled, chopped)
- 1 1/4 lb ground beef

Directions:

1. Add all of the ingredients to the slow cooker and mix well.

2. Place the lid on the slow cooker and choose the low setting. Cook for about 6 hours while stirring occasionally.

3. After cooking, transfer the dog food to a container and allow it to cool down completely before serving.

4. Store the leftovers in an airtight container, then place in the refrigerator or freezer.

MEATY MIX

Mixing different types of meat together can increase the protein content while making the dish more flavorful for your pup. Give this recipe a try and see the difference!

Time: *4 hours, 10 minutes* **Serving Size:** *7 servings* **Prep Time:** *10 minutes* **Cook Time:** *4 hours*	**Nutritional Facts:** **Calories:** *168kcal -* **Carbs:** *18.1g* **Fat:** *4.3g -* **Protein:** *14.2g*

Ingredients:

- 1/2 cup of brown rice (uncooked)
- 1/2 cup of kidney beans (canned, drained)
- 1/2 cup of mixed vegetables (frozen, thawed)
- 3/4 cup of water
- 1 1/2 lbs protein mix (combination of beef, fish, pork, and turkey or chicken)
- 1 egg
- 1 small apple (cored, chopped)
- 1 sweet potato (peeled, cut into chunks)

Directions:

1. In a bowl, add all of the meats and mix well.

2. Add the protein mix to the slow cooker along with the rest of the ingredients, and use a spatula to mix everything together.

3. Place the lid on the slow cooker and choose the high setting. Cook for about 4 hours while stirring occasionally.

4. After cooking, transfer the dog food to a container and allow it to cool down completely before serving.

5. Store the leftovers in an airtight container, then place in the refrigerator or freezer.

LEAN AND HEALTHY CHICKEN

This simple recipe is easy, healthy, and delicious for your four-legged friend. It features lean ground chicken for a good amount of protein without too much fat.

Time: *6 hours, 10 minutes* **Serving Size:** *4 servings* **Prep Time:** *10 minutes* **Cook Time:** *6 hours*	**Nutritional Facts:** **Calories:** *340kcal* - **Carbs:** *59.2g* **Fat:** *3.5g* - **Protein:** *19.1g*

Ingredients:

- 1 cup of butternut squash (peeled, cubed)
- 1 cup of green beans (canned, rinsed)
- 1 1/2 cups of brown rice (uncooked)
- 2 cups of kidney beans (canned, rinsed, drained)
- 1 cup of carrots (peeled, sliced)
- 1 cup of peas (canned, drained)
- 1 1/2 cups of water
- 1 lb ground chicken (lean)

Directions:

1. Add the water into the slow cooker, then add the rice. Mix well.

2. Add the rest of the ingredients and mix until well combined.

3. Place the lid on the slow cooker and choose the low setting. Cook for about 6 hours while stirring occasionally.

4. After cooking, transfer the dog food to a container and allow it to cool down completely before serving.

5. Store the leftovers in an airtight container, then place in the refrigerator or freezer.

POULTRY WITH A BIT OF SWEETNESS

If you want your furry pet to enjoy their meals, try different combinations to see which ones they like best. Maybe this interesting recipe will become your furry friend's new favorite!

Time: *12 hours, 15 minutes*	**Nutritional Facts:**
Serving Size: *9 servings*	**Calories:** *141kcal* - **Carbs:** *16.4g*
Prep Time: *15 minutes*	**Fat:** *3.2g* - **Protein:** *12.4g*
Cook Time: *12 hours*	

Ingredients:

- 1/2 cup of blueberries (frozen)
- 1/2 cup of peas (frozen)
- 1 1/2 lb ground turkey
- 1 sweet potato (diced)
- 1/2 cup of carrots (chopped)
- 1 1/2 lb chicken thighs (with skin and bones)
- 1 potato (diced)
- water (for cooking)

Directions:

1. Add the chicken into the slow cooker, then add enough water to submerge the meat completely. Add the rest of the ingredients and mix well.

2. Place the lid on the slow cooker and choose the low setting. Cook for about 12 hours while stirring occasionally.

3. After cooking, transfer the dog food to a container and remove all of the chicken bones.

4. Allow the dog food to cool down completely before serving.

5. Store the leftovers in an airtight container, then place in the refrigerator or freezer.

HEARTY BEEF STEW

Beef stew is a hearty dish that we all enjoy. Whip this dog-friendly version for your canine companion to warm them and fill them up on cold nights.

Time: *4 hours, 10 minutes*	**Nutritional Facts:**
Serving Size: *7 servings*	**Calories:** *71kcal -* **Carbs:** *9.6g*
Prep Time: *10 minutes*	**Fat:** *1g -* **Protein:** *5.6g*
Cook Time: *4 hours*	

Ingredients:

- 1/2 cup of carrots (diced)
- 1/2 cup of flour
- 1/2 cup of green beans (diced)
- 1/2 cup of water
- 1 lb of meat for beef stew (sliced)
- 1 sweet potato (diced)

Directions:

1. Add all of the ingredients into the slow cooker and mix until well combined.

2. Place the lid on the slow cooker and choose the high setting. Cook for about 4 hours while stirring occasionally.

3. After cooking, transfer the dog food to a container and allow it to cool down completely before serving.

4. Store the leftovers in an airtight container, then place in the refrigerator or freezer.

CHICKEN, FRUIT, AND VEGGIES

Mixing a healthy protein source with fruits and veggies will create a dog food dish that's both nutritious and filling for your furry best friend.

Time: *4 hours, 10 minutes* **Serving Size:** *7 servings* **Prep Time:** *10 minutes* **Cook Time:** *4 hours*	**Nutritional Facts:** **Calories:** *4012kcal* - **Carbs:** *15.5g* **Fat:** *21.4g* - **Protein:** *35g*

Ingredients:

- 1 cup of kidney beans (canned, drained)
- 1/4 lb chicken gizzards (roughly chopped)
- 1 lb chicken thighs (skinless, boneless, cut into cubes)
- 1 carrot (peeled, sliced)
- 1 sweet potato (diced)
- 2 cups of water
- 1/4 lb chicken livers (roughly chopped)
- 1 lb ground chicken
- 1 Granny Smith apple (cored, cut into chunks)

Directions:

1. Add all of the chicken into the slow cooker along with the carrots, beans, and sweet potatoes, and mix well.

2. Place the lid on the slow cooker and choose the high setting. Cook for about 4 hours while stirring occasionally.

3. After cooking, add the apple slices and mix well. Transfer the dog food to a container and allow it to cool down completely before serving.

4. Store the leftovers in an airtight container, then place in the refrigerator or freezer.

HERBED TURKEY

Herbs are filled with beneficial nutrients and they add flavor to food too. Adding herbs to your dog food recipes will surely make them taste better for your little doggie.

Time: *4 hours, 10 minutes* **Serving Size:** *5 servings* **Prep Time:** *10 minutes* **Cook Time:** *4 hours*	**Nutritional Facts:** **Calories:** *295kcal -***Carbs:** *53.1g* **Fat:** *6.5g -* **Protein:** *12.1g*

Ingredients:

- 1 tsp rosemary (dried)
- 1/2 cup of broccoli, carrots, and cauliflower mix (frozen, thawed)
- 2 cups of brown rice (uncooked)
- 6 cups of water
- 1 lb ground turkey

Directions:

1. Add the water into the slow cooker with the rice and mix well.

2. Add the rest of the ingredients and continue mixing until well combined.

3. Place the lid on the slow cooker and choose the high setting. Cook for about 4 hours while stirring occasionally.

4. After cooking, transfer the dog food to a container and allow it to cool down completely before serving.

5. Store the leftovers in an airtight container, then place in the refrigerator or freezer.

🐕 MEATLOAF FOR DOGGIES

You might be surprised with the title of this recipe, but dogs would love to have meatloaf too. Here is a recipe for doggy meatloaf to add to your furry friend's diet.

Time: 2 hours, 15 minutes	**Nutritional Facts:**
Serving Size: 6 servings	**Calories:** 243kcal - **Carbs:** 38.9g
Prep Time: 15 minutes	**Fat:** 4.8g - **Protein:** 13.8g
Cook Time: 2 hours	

Ingredients:

- 1/3 cup of tomato paste (canned)
- 1/2 cup of wheat germ
- 1 egg
- 1 small apple (cored, diced)
- 2 stalks of celery (chopped)
- 1/2 cup of rolled oats
- 3/4 lb ground beef (lean)
- 1 slice of white bread (torn into bite-sized pieces)
- 2 potatoes (cut into cubes)
- 3 carrots (peeled, grated)

Directions:

1. Preheat your slow cooker on high while you prepare the vegetables. In a bowl, add all of the ingredients and mix well.

2. Transfer the mixture to a roasting pan, then place the roasting pan in the preheated slow cooker.

3. Place the lid on the slow cooker. Cook on high for about 2 hours or until the meatloaf is completely cooked through.

4. After cooking, take the roasting pan out of the oven. Allow the meatloaf to cool down completely before slicing and serving. Store the leftover meatloaf in an airtight container, then place in the refrigerator or freezer.

BEEFY BONE BROTH

Bone broth is very nutritious as it contains all the nutrients from the ingredients it's made from. Your dog will surely love this flavorful broth that you can even add to other dishes to make them healthier.

Time: *9 hours, 10 minutes*	**Nutritional Facts:**
Serving Size: *12 servings*	**Calories:** *56kcal* - **Carbs:** *1g*
Prep Time: *10 minutes*	**Fat:** *6g* - **Protein:** *1g*
Cook Time: *9 hours*	

Ingredients:

- 6 cups of water
- 1 lb beef bones
- 1 carrot (chopped)
- 1 sprig of rosemary
- 1 stalk of celery (chopped)

Directions:

1. Add all of the water into the slow cooker.

2. Add the rest of the ingredients and mix well.

3. Place the lid on the slow cooker and choose the low setting. Cook for about 9 hours while stirring occasionally.

4. After cooking, use a slotted spoon to remove the bones and the sprig of rosemary.

5. Allow the broth to cool down completely before serving.

6. Store the leftovers in an airtight container, then place in the refrigerator or freezer.

🐕 OUTSTANDING OFFALS

Also known as organ meats, offals are a lot cheaper than meat. They contain a lot of nutrients, too, which makes them an excellent base ingredient for various dog food dishes.

Time: 5 hours, 10 minutes	**Nutritional Facts:**
Serving Size: 10 servings	**Calories:** 197kcal
Prep Time: 10 minutes	**Carbs:** 32.4g
Cook Time: 5 hours	**Fat:** 2.8g
	Protein: 12.2g

Ingredients:

- 1 cup of blueberries
- 1 1/2 cups of brown rice (uncooked)
- 2 cups of peas (frozen, thawed)
- 2 cups of spinach
- 1 lb organ meat like chicken gizzards, chicken hearts, beef or pork livers, etc.
- 2 apples (cored, sliced)
- 2 sweet potatoes (peeled, cut into cubes)
- 3 carrots (peeled, chopped)
- 1 butternut squash (peeled, cut into cubes)
- water (enough to fill the slow cooker)

Directions:

1. Add all of the ingredients into the slow cooker and pour enough water to cover everything completely.

2. Place the lid on the slow cooker and choose the low setting. Cook for about 5 hours while stirring occasionally.

3. After cooking, transfer the dog food to a container and allow it to cool down completely before serving.

4. Store the leftovers in an airtight container, then place in the refrigerator or freezer.

LIVER AND EGGS

If you've ever eaten liver and onions, you might want to cook this tasty dish for your doggy. Instead of onions, you will be adding eggs to make the dish more appealing to your canine's taste buds.

Time: *8 hours, 10 minutes* **Serving Size:** *8 servings* **Prep Time:** *10 minutes* **Cook Time:** *8 hours*	**Nutritional Facts:** **Calories:** *431kcal -* **Carbs:** *30g* **Fat:** *16g-* **Protein:** *40g*

Ingredients:

- 4 tbsp coconut oil
- 1 cup of brown rice (uncooked)
- 1 cup of Greek yogurt (plain)
- 2 cups of broccoli (cut into florets)
- 2 cups of carrots (peeled, chopped)
- 3 cups of water
- 2 lb beef liver
- 4 eggs

Directions:

1. Add the oil to the slow cooker and swirl it around to coat the bottom.

2. Add the rest of the ingredients to the slow cooker and mix to combine.

3. Place the lid on the slow cooker and choose the low setting. Cook for about 8 hours while stirring occasionally.

4. After cooking, transfer the liver and eggs to a container and allow it to cool down completely before serving.

5. Store the leftovers in an airtight container, then place in the refrigerator or freezer.

CHICKEN STEW

Chicken is a common ingredient in dog food recipes because it's palatable to canines. Make this stew for your furry friend, and watch their tail wag each time you serve it.

Time: *8 hours, 15 minutes*	**Nutritional Facts:**
Serving Size: *7 servings*	**Calories:** *138kcal*
Prep Time: *15 minutes*	**Carbs:** *8.3g*
Cook Time: *8 hours*	**Fat:** *8.7g*
	Protein: *8.1g*

Ingredients:

- 1/2 tbsp olive oil
- 1/8 cup of chicken liver
- 1/2 cup of green beans (frozen, thawed)
- 1/2 cup of peas (frozen, thawed)

- 2 cups of water
- 1 1/2 lb chicken thighs (boneless, skinless)
- 1 apple (cored, sliced)
- 1 carrot (peeled, sliced)
- a handful of parsley (fresh, chopped)

Directions:

1. Add the chicken thighs to the slow cooker along with the chicken livers, apples, green beans, carrots, and water, then mix everything together well.

2. Place the lid on the slow cooker and choose the low setting. Cook for about 8 hours while stirring occasionally.

3. Around 15 minutes before the end of the cooking time, add the olive oil, parsley, and peas. Mix well and continue cooking.

4. After cooking, transfer the dog food to a container and allow it to cool down completely before serving.

5. Store the leftovers in an airtight container, then place in the refrigerator or freezer.

🐕 BEEF AND PORK

Combining different types of meat to create dishes for your pet could make their diet more diverse. Here is an example of such a recipe where you would combine pork and chicken in one dish!

Time: *7 hours, 15 minutes*	**Nutritional Facts:**
Serving Size: *8 servings*	**Calories:** *100kcal* - **Carbs:** *13.5g*
Prep Time: *15 minutes*	**Fat:** *1.5g* - **Protein:** *8.2g*
Cook Time: *7 hours*	

Ingredients:

- 1/2 cup of brown rice (uncooked)
- 3/4 cup of water
- 1 lb ground pork
- 1 apple (cored, cut into cubes)
- 1 sweet potato (peeled, cut into cubes)
- 1/2 cup of kale (tough stems removed, chopped)
- 1 lb ground beef
- 1/4 cup of blueberries
- 1 carrot (peeled, cut into chunks)

Directions:

1. Add all of the ingredients to the slow cooker and mix everything together.

2. Place the lid on the slow cooker and choose the low setting. Cook for about 7 hours while stirring occasionally.

3. After cooking, transfer the dog food to a container and allow it to cool down completely before serving. Store the leftovers in an airtight container, then place in the refrigerator or freezer.

DUCK WITH VEGGIES

Chicken isn't the only poultry that dogs like to eat. Giving your furry friend duck once in a while will surely make them appreciate you more. Here is a tasty duck recipe for you.

Time: *4 hours, 10 minutes*	**Nutritional Facts:**
Serving Size: *8 servings*	**Calories:** *175kcal*
Prep Time: *10 minutes*	**Carbs:** *33.8g*
Cook Time: *4 hours*	**Fat:** *1.6g*
	Protein: *6.3g*

Ingredients:

- 1 cup of carrots (peeled, diced)
- 1 cup of celery (diced)
- 1 cup of potato (peeled, diced)
- 1 cup of pumpkin (peeled, diced)
- 1 cup of zucchini (peeled, diced)
- 3 cups of brown rice (uncooked)
- 1 duck breast (boneless, skinless, diced)
- water (enough to fill the slow cooker)

Directions:

1. Add all of the ingredients into the slow cooker and pour enough water to cover everything completely.

2. Place the lid on the slow cooker and choose the low setting. Cook for about 4 hours while stirring occasionally.

3. After cooking, transfer the dog food to a container and allow it to cool down completely before serving.

4. Store the leftovers in an airtight container, then place in the refrigerator or freezer.

🐕 HEARTY GROUND TURKEY

Turkey is another type of poultry you can use to make delicious food for your dog. This recipe also includes different vegetables to make the meal more satisfying.

Time: *3 hours, 5 minutes*	**Nutritional Facts:**
Serving Size: *10 servings*	**Calories:** *142kcal* - **Carbs:** *14g*
Prep Time: *5 minutes*	**Fat:** *1g* - **Protein:** *17g*
Cook Time: *3 hours*	

Ingredients:

- 1/2 cup of green beans (fresh, chopped)
- 3/4 cup of carrot (peeled, chopped)
- 1 cup of kidney beans (canned, drained, rinsed)
- 1 1/2 lb ground turkey
- 3/4 cup of brown rice (uncooked)
- 3/4 cup of sweet potato (peeled, chopped)
- 1 3/4 cups of water

Directions:

1. Add all of the ingredients into the slow cooker and mix well.

2. Place the lid on the slow cooker and choose the high setting. Cook for about 3 hours while stirring occasionally.

3. After cooking, transfer the dog food to a container and allow it to cool down completely before serving.

4. Store the leftovers in an airtight container, then place in the refrigerator or freezer.

BEEFY BROCCOLI

Beef and broccoli go perfectly together. You can even whip up this combination for your canine companion to add flavor and nutrition to their diet.

Time: 6 hours, 10 minutes	**Nutritional Facts:**
Serving Size: 10 servings	**Calories:** 281kcal - **Carbs:** 18.5g
Prep Time: 10 minutes	**Fat:** 21.3g - **Protein:** 5.8g
Cook Time: 6 hours	

Ingredients:

- 2 tbsp coconut oil
- 1 cup of water
- 2 cups of brown rice (uncooked)
- 1 carrot (peeled, sliced)
- 1 cup of Greek yogurt (plain)
- 2 cups of broccoli (cut into florets
- 1 lb beef liver

Directions:

1. Add all of the ingredients into the slow cooker and mix well.

2. Place the lid on the slow cooker and choose the medium setting. Cook for about 6 hours while stirring occasionally.

3. After cooking, transfer the dog food to a container and allow it to cool down completely before serving.

4. Store the leftovers in an airtight container, then place in the refrigerator or freezer.

STEWED SWEET POTATOES

You may have noticed how sweet potatoes are a common ingredient in dog food recipes. You can even use it as the main ingredient to make a nutrient-rich and flavorful dish for your canine companion.

Time: *4 hours, 10 minutes*	**Nutritional Facts:**
Serving Size: *10 servings*	**Calories:** *231kcal*
Prep Time: *10 minutes*	**Carbs:** *41.2g*
Cook Time: *4 hours*	**Fat:** *2.6g*
	Protein: *11.2g*

Ingredients:

- 1 cup of kidney beans (canned, drained, rinsed)
- 1 cup of lentils (uncooked)
- 1 cup of oats (uncooked)
- 1 cup of peas (frozen, thawed)
- 2 cups of brown rice (uncooked)
- 1 lb ground turkey
- 2 sweet potatoes (peeled, cut into cubes)

Directions:

1. Add all of the ingredients into the slow cooker and mix to combine.

2. Place the lid on the slow cooker and choose the high setting. Cook for about 4 hours while stirring occasionally.

3. After cooking, transfer the dog food to a container and allow it to cool down completely before serving.

4. Store the leftovers in an airtight container, then place in the refrigerator or freezer.

MAKE YOUR OWN RECIPE

After trying to make different variations of dog food recipes, you can start making your own recipe based on your observation of your pet's preferences.

Time: depends on the main protein that you use **Serving Size:** 12 servings	**Nutritional Facts:** depends on the ingredients you use

Ingredients:

- 2 tbsp coconut oil
- 1/2 cup of fruit (peeled and cored apples, blueberries, etc.)
- 2 cups of greens (spinach, kale, lettuce, etc.)
- 2 cups of mixed vegetables (peas, carrots, sweet potato, broccoli, etc.)
- 3 lb meat (beef, pork, turkey, chicken, duck, offals, or a combination)
- water (as needed)

Directions:

1. Add all of the ingredients into the slow cooker and mix well.

2. Place the lid on the slow cooker and choose the proper setting. Cook while stirring occasionally. The cooking time will depend on the ingredients you choose and the setting of your slow cooker.

3. After cooking, transfer the dog food to a container and allow it to cool down completely before serving.

4. Store the leftovers in an airtight container, then place in the refrigerator or freezer.

CONCLUSION:
NOURISHING FOUR-LEGGED LOVE, EVERY DAY

There you have it!

Everything you need to know to start cooking homemade food for your beloved pet. If this is your first time to whip up your own doggy treats at home, you are now armed with a wealth of information to make the process easier for you.

As promised at the beginning of this cookbook, you have learned the fundamentals of using a slow cooker to cook various dog recipes, along with other valuable information. We started off by understanding why home-cooked food is the better option for your canine companion compared to industrial dog food. While commercial products come with a lot of promises, starting with fresh ingredients to create nutritious dishes for your pet is more beneficial in the long run.

Then, we delved into the world of cooking, where you discovered the basic tools needed to make home-cooked food. In this chapter, you also found out the fundamentals of slow cookers, how they work, and how you can use them to make delicious and nutritious doggy meals. The same chapter also included tips for how to choose the best ingredients for your dog food recipes, along with the common mistakes to avoid when using a slow cooker for the task.

The next thing you discovered was the nutritional value of ingredients and how important it is to understand these values to make sure that you're always giving your pup the best food ever. This chapter also contained tips for how to give your pet the right portion sizes, plus some useful conversion charts that will help make cooking easier for you. Then, we moved on to the proper ways of storing the food that you have made for your pet. Since you will be cooking dog food in big batches, you need to know how to store the bulk of that food so that you can quickly thaw, reheat, and serve it at every meal.

The last chapter contained a bunch of recipes for you to start off with. These recipes feature different proteins so that your dog can enjoy different textures and flavors. Make sure to follow the recipes carefully, especially when you're just beginning your journey of making home-cooked food for your furry friend. Practice making these recipes first, and when you get the hang of using your slow cooker to make food for your pet, then you can start thinking about making your own recipes.

Throughout this book, you have discovered so much useful information that you can now apply to your own life. Your pet will surely thank you once you transition them from eating commercial dog food to homemade meals, which are more nutritious and potentially a lot tastier too.

Now that you have reached the end of the book, the only thing left to do is to use what you have learned. Create a plan and a menu, then start shopping for ingredients! Being a pet parent will feel a lot more fulfilling if you can help your pet become healthier by healing them from the inside out.

SOME TESTIMONIALS FROM FUR PARENTS LIKE YOU AND ME!

Before writing this book, I had helped a bunch of friends and family discover the wonders of using a slow cooker to make dog food at home. Then, my loved ones branched out and told other people about their wonderful journeys, which led them to come to me for guidance as well.

If you're still on the fence in terms of deciding to cook for your pet or if you just want to feel better about your decision to become your pet's own personal chef, take a look at these wonderful testimonials that I received!

> *I always thought that cooking food for my beloved pet would be too difficult. I had never even thought about using a slow cooker to make dog food! Once I learned, I discovered how simple it was, and as I helped my Travis transition to eating home-cooked meals, I saw all the wonderful benefits right before my eyes.* -**Kelly, 32**

> *Years ago, I bought a slow cooker to make healthy meals for my kids. Then, I found out that I could also use it to make high-quality meals for my pet. Once I started, I just couldn't stop because it was so fun and easy.* -**Jonathan, 28**

> *Cooking for my Binky has made her so happy and healthy. I found out from my best friend that she started whipping up healthy meals for her dogs, and I didn't want to be left behind. So, I also discovered what I needed to do, and I've been a lot happier ever since.* -**Iris, 22**

> *Whenever I fed my dog those dog food products in supermarkets, I always wondered if they were healthy enough. Now I know that homemade food is a lot healthier and I decided to make the switch. All pet parents should make the same decision, especially if they want their doggies to stay strong and healthy.* -**Naomi, 40**

I'm a big fan of meal planning, and when I learned that I could also do this for my dog Toby, I got super excited! Now, I make menus for my family and for Toby, too. I've been making the most of my slow cooker, which is a great benefit as I never really used it since I got it. It has become one of my most valuable appliances at home now! **-Derek, 25**

BONUS CHAPTER:
DEALING WITH CHALLENGES WHEN COOKING DOG FOOD AT HOME

Cooking food for your dog can become a fun and relaxing chore. But helping your pup transition to home-cooked meals might not be as easy, especially at the beginning. You might encounter a number of challenges, which could make you feel discouraged or overwhelmed. But knowing how to handle these difficult situations will keep you motivated to keep going. So here's a bonus chapter to help you out!

THE MOST COMMON CHALLENGES AND HOW TO DEAL WITH THEM

As you have learned, cooking your dog's food can be beneficial to them. If you have a slow cooker at home, the process can even be easy, time-saving, and economical. However, cooking your dog's meals and helping them change their diet might not be as easy or simple as you might hope. You may encounter some challenges along the way. The good news is that being aware of these challenges will help you overcome them effectively.

Nutrient Deficiencies

One of the biggest challenges in changing your dog's diet is the potential for developing nutrient deficiencies. Although commercial dog food products may contain unnecessary or potentially harmful ingredients, the makers of these products have researched the appropriate nutrients dogs need. High-quality dog food products may contain a good balance of nutrients to keep your dog healthy. If you don't plan your pet's meals well, you might experience issues like:

- Not enough protein or not getting enough good protein if you only use one type of protein source all the time.

- Getting incomplete proteins if you only focus on plant-based protein sources.

- An imbalance of minerals such as calcium, phosphorus, and more.

- Not getting enough vitamin A, vitamin D, B vitamins, and more, which could cause a number of health issues.

Sadly, some recipes out there don't contain enough nutrients because the ingredients they contain aren't well balanced. Always remember that dogs have very specific nutritional needs, which is why you need to know exactly what goes into your child's meals. If you can do this, then you won't have to worry about your pup suffering from nutrient deficiencies.

Adding Potentially Harmful Ingredients

While you can add virtually any kind of ingredients to your meals as long as you or your family members don't have allergies or food intolerance, this isn't the same for dogs. You need to be more careful when including some types of food in your pet's meals because some ingredients can be potentially harmful to them. Here are some examples:

- Avocados could cause diarrhea and vomiting and even have adverse effects on your dog's heart.

- Chocolate could cause toxicity to your dog's central nervous system, heart issues, and gastrointestinal issues.

- Chives, onions, and garlic could damage your dog's red blood cells and cause gastrointestinal issues.

- Raisins and grapes could cause kidney failure and even damage your dog's liver.

- Macadamia nuts could have adverse effects on your dog's nervous system and muscles.

- Bones that have been cooked could splinter when chewed and puncture your dog's insides or even cause choking when not chewed properly.

- Foods that contain xylitol could damage your dog's liver and even cause hypoglycemia.

- Alcohol is toxic to your dog, even in small amounts, as it could cause diarrhea, incoordination, and other health issues.

Even proteins that contain too much fat could be harmful to your dog when added to their meals often. This is why it's better to choose lean proteins in your dog food recipes, as these are more nutritious. If you want to be sure, you can always go online and research the ingredients of dog food recipes to make sure that everything they contain is safe. This is the best way to make sure that you're not giving your pup anything that could compromise their health.

Considering All Factors Related to Your Dog's Health

The food your dog eats isn't the only thing you need to consider while transitioning them into a new diet. While it is important to make sure that you are feeding your pet a nutrient-dense, balanced diet, there are other factors you need to think about, too. These include:

- Any specific health issues your dog might have as these could have an effect on their nutritional needs. Have your pet checked to find out if they suffer from any kind of medical condition?

- Giving your dog additional supplements if you feel that the food they eat doesn't contain enough nutrients.

- Varying your dog's meals so that they don't get tired of eating the same thing over and over again. Eventually, your pup might stop eating altogether.

When in doubt, the best thing you could do is to consult your vet. Have your dog checked and ask about their nutritional needs. You may also want to continue to monitor your dog's health, especially during the transition phase.

Other Common Challenges

The truth is that all dogs transition in different ways. Just as you would need to adjust to a new diet, your dog would need a period of adjustment, too. Educating yourself by understanding the common challenges you might encounter would make it easier for you to deal with them as they come. Other common challenges include:

- Only feeding your dog meat and vegetables might cause nutrient deficiencies. This is why it's a good idea to include fruits, other carbohydrate sources, and even supplements to your dog's diet if needed.

- Feeding your dog under-cooked or raw food isn't always safe, as these might contain bacteria that could make your pet sick.

- Not checking the dog food recipes you find from various sources could be dangerous as the recipes might contain harmful ingredients.

- Not customizing the recipes to suit your pup's needs would prevent them from getting all of the potential benefits of home-cooked meals. Customizing the recipes for your pet means taking into consideration their age, breed, size, food allergies or intolerance, the existence of medical conditions, and nutritional needs.

You also have the option to consult with an animal nutritionist to make sure that you're giving your pet everything they need in terms of their diet. Keeping yourself informed throughout the process is the best way to ensure that your dog stays happy and healthy, and lives a long life.

SAFETY PRECAUTIONS TO KEEP IN MIND

One of the main reasons why you may have chosen to cook your dog's food yourself would be to help them become happier and healthier. This is an excellent reason. But if you don't cook your dog's food properly, you might end up giving them something that could cause adverse effects on their health. You can ensure your pet's safety by being aware of these safety concerns.

Food Contamination

All food is prone to contamination. The good thing about the food that we eat is that we keep them in pots, pans, serving bowls, and serving platters. And when you eat, you place your food on clean plates. If you want to avoid food contamination, you may want to do the same for your dog. After cooking their meals in a slow cooker, transfer them to a clean bowl to cool down. When it's time to store your dog's food, place individual portions in airtight containers or resealable bags. All of these will reduce the risk of bacteria getting into your dog's food, which would keep it safe to eat for your pet.

Adding Foods That Contain Allergens

If you know that you or one of your loved ones is allergic to any type of food or has any kind of food intolerance, you will make sure not to feed them that food. To keep your pet safe, do this for them, too. As you transition your pet to home-cooked meals, observe their reactions. If you notice any adverse effects, find out what food causes those effects so that you can keep those out of your pet's meals. Allergens don't belong in your dog's diet, so make sure that nothing like that goes into your pet's recipes.

Other Potential Safety Concerns

Aside from preventing contamination and the risk of allergens, there are other potential safety concerns you should consider. Taking all of these into account will keep your pet healthy and safe:

- Never include human-safe ingredients that contain compounds that are toxic to dogs. Remember to do your research, especially when trying out new recipes.

- Wash your hands first before you handle your dog's food, whether during the cooking stage or during the reheating and serving stages.

- Throw out any spoiled ingredients.

- Check your dog's food stored food before serving it.

- Always check your sources before using a recipe. If you can't find the source of the recipes, check the list of ingredients to make sure that everything is safe for your dog to eat.

- Avoid feeding your dog meals that are too fatty, rich, or might contain exotic ingredients that you don't even eat.

- Make sure to follow the recipes, especially in terms of the quantity of ingredients and the cooking times.

Practicing food safety when cooking meals for your pet is your responsibility. Aside from all of the tips mentioned above, you also need to make sure that you're feeding your pet all of the nutrients they need based on their breed, age, and current health status.

Find a time to prepare big batches of dog food, then store the leftovers properly in the refrigerator or freezer. This will make it easier for you to follow through instead of jumping from home-cooked meals to commercial dog food products randomly. Avoid this, as it could make it difficult for your pet to get used to eating the food that you cook. Plan your pet's meals well, and practice these safety tips each time you cook so you won't have to worry about your pet's health.

FEEDING A PICKY EATER

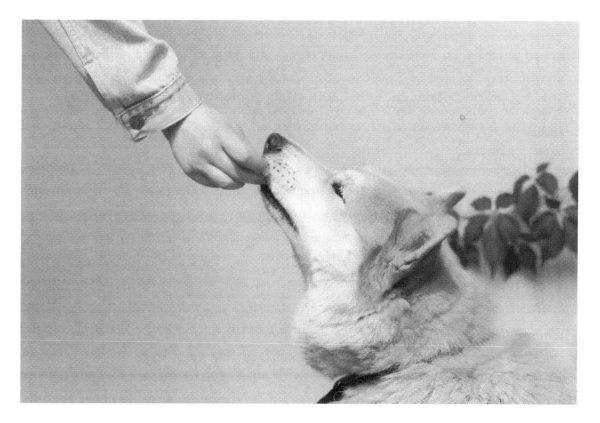

Surprising as it might seem, some dogs can be picky eaters, too. A lot of people think that canines would just scarf down anything in front of them, but this isn't always true. There are many reasons why dogs become picky eaters, and if you discover that it's very challenging to get your pup to eat, there are things you can do to overcome this.

Establish a Feeding Routine for Your Dog

Training dogs involves a lot of steps, but if you can do this, living with your pet becomes a lot easier. In order to encourage your pet to eat what you feed them, establishing a feeding routine is essential. Find out the best time to feed your dog. This could take some trial and error, but if you can find the perfect time, mealtimes won't have to be so challenging.

Place your dog's bowl out and see if they will eat. Leave it there for up to half an hour, then take it away. Don't leave your dog's food sitting on the floor for longer than that as it could cause their food to spoil. A few hours later, try again. The act of taking your pet's food away helps them learn that they need to eat their food when you serve it.

Find the Best Place for Your Dog to Eat

The right location could be helpful too and this could be part of your dog's feeding routine. Try placing your dog's bowl in different places to see if there is a location where they prefer to eat. If you can find a good spot that won't cause any issues for anyone in your household, keep feeding your pet in that place.

Choose the Best Bowl for Your Dog

This might not seem very important, but having the right bowl can encourage your picky eater to eat everything you serve. Avoid using a plastic bowl, as this material can affect the taste and smell of your dog's food. Plastic bowls are also difficult to clean, and if you don't do this well, they might harbor bacteria that could contaminate the food you put into the bowl.

The material of the bowl isn't the only factor to consider. If you have an older dog, you may want a raised bowl so they can eat easily. If your dog is flat-faced, choose a bowl that is specifically designed for those types of dogs as it might be difficult for them to eat everything, especially around the edges of standard food bowls. Observe how your dog eats from their bowl to see if you need to change it to improve the way they eat.

Experiment With Different Textures and Flavors

Sometimes, picky eaters just need some encouragement in order to discover how yummy your home-cooked meals are. This is especially true if you are changing your dog's food from commercial dog food to home-cooked dog food. Challenging as it might be to watch your dog reject the food you cook every single day, you can try experimenting with different textures and flavors to see what would appeal to your pet. You can even mix some kibble into your home-cooked meals at the beginning so that they smell and taste something familiar in their food. Varying the tastes and textures could also help your dog feel excited about mealtimes, which would reduce their pickiness.

Add Tasty Toppers to Help Your Dog Get Used to Home-Cooked Meals

Adding toppers to your dog's meals can make your pet feel happier and more excited about mealtimes. Dry kibble is the most common choice as the crunchy bits would make it fun for your dog to chew their food. Another option is to add human food as long as you know that it's safe for your pet to eat. Some examples of human food toppers you can add to your meals include yogurt, cooked eggs, some cheese, peanut butter, and the like.

Observe what food toppers your dog really likes so you can add those when you see that your pet is being a bit picky. Also, rotate the toppers so your pet won't get tired of them. As time goes by, you can reduce the frequency of placing these additions to your dog's meals until they get used to eating the food you cook without needing any enhancements.

Avoid Giving Your Dog Table Scraps or Doggy Treats

While it's okay to top your dog's meals with human food once in a while, avoid giving them scraps from your table during your meal times. Giving your picky eater food when it's not time for them to eat will only make the issue worse. Aside from getting full from the table scraps and treats, your pet will learn that they don't have to eat the food in their bowl since you will give them food from your plate anyway.

Remember to Consider Potential Food Sensitivity

In some cases, picky dogs have food sensitivities, which is why they don't eat what's served to them. Apart from the common allergens and foods that aren't suitable for dogs, some common ingredients that could cause food sensitivities include dairy products, chicken, eggs, beef, corn, soy, wheat gluten, and some additives. This is why you need to keep observing your pet, especially when you are transitioning them to home-cooked food. If you find out that your pet is only rejecting meals with certain ingredients, then you may have to avoid using those ingredients.

Make Your Dog Hungry Before Feeding

Another way to encourage your dog to eat what you serve them is by getting them to exercise. All dogs need to live an active lifestyle. They need to run, play, and do other types of physical activity each day such as walking to the park, playing fetch, obedience training, and more. Getting your pet to do these activities would make them hungry, which then makes them feel more excited about finishing the food in their bowls.

Warm Up Your Dog's Food

You may try warming up your dog's food before serving it as this may enhance the flavors. If you notice that your pet likes eating food that has been freshly cooked compared to food that comes from the refrigerator, even if it has been thawed, this tip might work to reduce your pet's pickiness.

Make Mealtime Fun

You may have noticed how your dog really likes to play. In some cases, instead of eating their food, dogs will just play with the contents of their bowl. To encourage your pet to eat, make mealtimes more fun for them. Invest in playthings like a snuffle mat, a puzzle feeder, or a food bowl. That way, your pup will have to work for their food and get a tasty reward each time. Whenever your pet is able to finish all of its food after playing, reward it with good words and hugs. This will make your pet even happier that they finished their food.

Don't Rush Into Things

Finally, it's a good thing to take things slow so your pet doesn't feel overwhelmed. Your pup may already be used to commercial dog food and becoming picky when served with something unfamiliar is quite a common reaction. To avoid this, change your dog's food little by little and do it one day at a time. This will make it easier for your dog to adjust without learning to reject the food that you cook for them.

REFERENCES

Aimee. (2023, February 12). *Essential kitchen tools for cooking*. Simple Bites. https://simplebites.net/essential-kitchen-tools-for-cooking/

All about dog food - Feeding guide. (n.d.). All about Dog Food. https://www.allaboutdogfood.co.uk/dog-feeding-guide

Alli. (2019, August 12). *How to use a slow cooker*. Longbourn Farm. https://longbournfarm.com/how-to-use-a-slow-cooker/

Alonge, J. (2023, May 9). How to make homemade dog food: Risks & considerations. *Ollie Blog*. https://blog.myollie.com/homemade-dog-food/

Avoiding the biggest mistake when home cooking for your dog. (2023, February 3). *Dog Child*. https://dogchild.co/blogs/learn/avoiding-the-biggest-mistake-when-home-cooking-for-your-dog

Bast, J. (2023, October 11). Risks of home cooking for your dog. *Ollie Blog*. https://blog.myollie.com/risks-of-home-cooking-for-your-dog/

A beginner's guide to home cooking for dogs. (2018, November 20). *Union Lake Veterinary Hospital*. https://unionlakeveterinaryhospital.com/blog/a-beginners-guide-to-home-cooking-for-dogs

The big problem with commercial dog foods. (2023, July 11). *ChefPaw*. https://www.chefpaw.com/blogs/news/the-big-problem-with-commercial-dog-foods

Bocco, D. (2023, November 11). Homemade dog food: A super guide for everything you need to know + 10 Recipes. *Cola's Kitchen*. https://colaskitchen.com/blog-posts/homemade-dog-food-a-super-guide-for-everything-you-need-to-know-10-recipes

Brunotts, K. (2022, January 4). *7 Best crockpot recipes for dogs*. K9 of Mine. https://www.k9ofmine.com/slow-cooker-crockpot-dog-food-recipes/

Casey, E. (n.d.). *Homemade dog food*. Slow Cooker Central. https://www.slowcookercentral.com/recipe/homemade-dog-food-2/

Chewy Editorial. (2017, April 1). *5 Mistakes to avoid when cooking for your dog*. Be Chewy. https://be.chewy.com/nutrition-food-treats-5-mistakes-to-avoid-when-cooking-for-your-dog/

Chungah. (2015, May 14). *Easy crockpot dog food*. Damn Delicious. https://damndelicious.net/2015/05/13/easy-crockpot-dog-food/

Coates, J. (2020, May 5). *Are you feeding your dog the right amount?* PetMD. https://www.petmd.com/dog/nutrition/are-you-feeding-your-dog-right-amount

Cooking tools and utensils. (2023, December 4). *The New York Times*. https://www.nytimes.com/wirecutter/kitchen-dining/tools-kitchen-dining/

Crenshaw, K. (2017, July 3). *Homemade dog food crockpot recipe with ground chicken*. A Fork's Tale. https://www.aforkstale.com/easy-homemade-crockpot-dog-food/

Dody. (n.d.). Slow cooker dog food. *Holistic Vet Blend*. https://holisticvetblend.com/blogs/news/slow-cooker-dog-food

Dog food calculator - How much & how often. (n.d.). Pedigree. https://www.pedigree.com.ph/feeding/feeding-calculator

Dos and don'ts of making homemade dog food. (2023, January 11). *Neater Pets*. https://neaterpets.com/blogs/news/dos-and-donts-homemade-dog-food

Downs, A. (2022, April 22). *5 Best crockpot dog food recipes (Step-by-step guide)*. Top Dog Tips. https://topdogtips.com/best-crockpot-dog-food-recipes/

Easy slow-cooker dog food. (n.d.). Bell & Evans. https://www.bellandevans.com/recipe/easy-slow-cooker-dog-food/

English, K. (2023, June 19). Unlocking the flavourful magic of slow cookers. *DID Electrical*. https://www.did.ie/blogs/cooking/unlocking-the-flavorful-magic-of-slow-cookers

Essential dog food ingredients for healthy dogs. (2023, August 9). Toronto North Animal Hospital. https://www.tnah.ca/why-are-dog-food-ingredients-important/

Feeding guidelines. (n.d.). Pedigree. https://www.pedigree.com.ph/feeding/feeding-guidelines

5 Of the biggest problems with commercial dog food – and what to do about it! (n.d.). *Wellbeing for Dogs.* https://wellbeingfordogs.com.au/blogs/wellbeing/5-of-the-biggest-problems-with-dog-food-and-what-to-do-about-it

Getting started with homemade dog food. (n.d.). Hearthstone Homemade Dog Food. https://www.hearthstonehomemadedogfood.com/getting-started-with-diy-dog-food

Ghosh, S. (2022, November 10). *A complete beginner's guide to making balanced homecooked dog food.* LinkedIn. https://www.linkedin.com/pulse/complete-beginners-guide-making-balanced-homecooked-dog-ghosh?trk=public_profile_article_view

Groshek, N. (2023, June 29). *11 Tips for feeding a picky dog.* Stella & Chewy's. https://www.stellaandchewys.com/dogs/picky-eater/

Gwen. (2016, May 5). *Crock pot dog food.* Slow Cooker Kitchen. https://www.slowcookerkitchen.com/crock-pot-dog-food/

Hardin, B. (2017, July 6). *Basic cooking measurements & handy kitchen conversion chart.* The Cookie Rookie. https://www.thecookierookie.com/cooking-measurements-kitchen-conversion-chart/

Healthy dog food toppers for picky eaters. (2023, June 5). Very Important Paws. https://www.veryimportantpaws.com/healthy-dog-food-toppers-for-picky-eaters/

Higashiyama, K. (2022, February 10). *How to make beef bone broth for dogs.* The Heirloom Pantry. https://theheirloompantry.co/how-to-make-beef-bone-broth-for-dogs/

Homemade crockpot dog food. (2020, May 21). Happy & Handcrafted. https://happyandhandcrafted.com/homemade-crockpot-dog-food/

Homemade dog food ingredients: 3 Essential foods for dogs. (n.d.). Posh Dog Knee Brace. https://poshdogkneebrace.com/dog-food-ingredients-3-essential-foods/?gad_source=1&gclid=EAIaIQobChMIuezGy-2AhQMVg6dmAh3ptQ7REAMYASAAEgLkcfD_BwE

Homemade dog food: What to include & what to avoid. (n.d.). Purina. https://www.purina.co.uk/articles/dogs/feeding/guides/homemade-dog-food

Homemade pet food guidance: Teaching clients to avoid common pitfalls and maintain quality control. (2021, March 4). AAHA. https://www.aaha.org/publications/newstat/articles/2021-03/homemade-pet-food-guidance-teaching-clients-to-avoid-common-pitfalls-and-maintain-quality-control/

Homemade vs. commercial dog food: Making the best nutritional choice. (2023, October 24). *PureForm Pet Health Supplements.* https://pureformpethealth.com/blogs/pureform-pet-care/homemade-vs-commercial-dog-food-making-the-best-nutritional-choice

How to make homemade dog food. (n.d.). *Know Better Pet Food.* https://www.knowbetterpetfood.com/blogs/blog/how-to-make-homemade-dog-food

How to store homemade dog food. (n.d.). *Opal Pets.* https://opalpets.com/blogs/news/how-to-store-homemade-dog-food

Iacono, G. (2023, July 26). *How to store homemade dog food: 6 Vet-approved tips.* Hepper. https://www.hepper.com/how-to-store-homemade-dog-food/

Kawczynska, C. (2021, July 13). *3 Reasons to cook your own dog food.* The Wildest. https://www.thewildest.com/dog-nutrition/reasons-make-your-own-dog-food

Kearl, M. (2024, February 16). *Cooking For your dog: Pros and cons of cooking homemade dog food.* American Kennel Club. https://www.akc.org/expert-advice/nutrition/cooking-for-your-dog-dos-and-donts/

Kimberly. (2020, November 28). *Crock pot dog food.* Canine Crazies. https://caninecrazies.com/crock-pot-dog-food/

Knerl, L. (n.d.). *Make homemade dog food with your slow-cooker.* Wise Bread. https://www.wisebread.com/make-homemade-dog-food-with-your-slow-cooker

Krista. (2019, October 24). *Slow cooker homemade dog food.* The Hungry Lyoness. https://thehungrylyoness.com/slow-cooker-homemade-dog-food/

Llera, R., & Yuill, C. (2009). *Nutrition - General feeding guidelines for dogs.* VCA.

https://vcahospitals.com/know-your-pet/nutrition-general-feeding-guidelines-for-dogs

Meyers, H. (2024, February 2). *Homemade dog food recipes: Choosing balanced ingredients*. American Kennel Club. https://www.akc.org/expert-advice/nutrition/choosing-ingredients-homemade-dog-food/

Middleton, J. (2023, May 26). Dog food storage: All you need to know. *James & Ella*. https://ella.co/blog/dog-food-storage

msmia. (n.d.). *Homemade dog food in the crockpot recipe*. Food. https://www.food.com/recipe/homemade-dog-food-in-the-crockpot-517180

NCCF Staff. (2024, February 5). Homemade dog food benefits & risks for your pup. *The National Canine Cancer Foundation*. https://wearethecure.org/blog/homemade-dog-food-benefits-and-risks/

Nowak, K. (2020, March 2). How much should I feed my dog? *The Dog People by Rover.com*. https://www.rover.com/blog/how-much-should-i-feed-my-dog/

OVRS Staff. (2021, January 1). Nutritious and delicious: Your guide to homemade dog food. *Oakland Veterinary Referral Services*. https://www.ovrs.com/blog/homemade-dog-food/

Pepin, G. (2023, January 8). *Batch cooking for dogs*. The Canine Nutritionist. https://www.caninenutritionist.co.uk/food-feeding/batch-cooking-for-dogs/

PoochWell. (2023a, April 6). *Can the commercial dog food: Why homemade canned dog food is the way to go!* Medium. https://medium.com/@bulldoglove/can-the-commercial-dog-food-why-homemade-canned-dog-food-is-the-way-to-go-180e3957e3c2

PoochWell. (2023b, April 9). *From fridge to freezer: How to store homemade dog food like a pro*. Medium. https://medium.com/@bulldoglove/from-fridge-to-freezer-how-to-store-homemade-dog-food-like-a-pro-b64fb418f04d

Randall, S. (2023, July 30). *Homemade beef and pork crock pot dog food recipe (Cheap and easy)*. Top Dog Tips. https://topdogtips.com/beef-and-pork-dog-food-recipe/

Recipe for homemade beef stew for your dog. (2015, February 11). Love and Kisses Pet Sitting, NC.

https://loveandkissespetsitting.net/homemade-beef-stew-for-your-dog/

Red Girl. (2023, November 12). *Homemade dog food recipe*. Allrecipes. https://www.allrecipes.com/recipe/140286/homemade-dog-food/

Sara. (2023, November 15). *23 Tricks to get a picky dog to eat his food (Every last bit!)*. Dog Lab. https://doglab.com/dog-not-eating/

Second Chance Baker . (2021, August 31). *Doggy meatloaf with vegetables*. Allrecipes. https://www.allrecipes.com/recipe/140483/doggy-meatloaf-with-vegetables/

7 Things you need to know about slow cookers. (n.d.). Cook with Campbells Canada. https://www.cookwithcampbells.ca/articles/7-things-need-know-slow-cookers/

The shocking truth about commercial dog food. (2015, January 10). Dog Food Advisor. https://www.dogfoodadvisor.com/dog-food-industry-exposed/shocking-truth-about-dog-food/

Splawn, M. (2022, December 19). *5 Essential things you should know about using your slow cooker*. The Spruce Eats. https://www.thespruceeats.com/essential-things-about-using-slow-cooker-6744668

Subbiah, K. (2023, June 22). Understanding dog food: Its ingredients & importance. *Supertails*. https://supertails.com/blogs/nutrition/understanding-dog-food-its-ingredients-importance

The National Academies. (2006). *A science-based guide for pet owners*. https://nap.nationalacademies.org/resource/10668/dog_nutrition_final_fix.pdf

The tail-wagging trend of homemade dog food: A guide to cooking for your canine companion. (2023, December 29). *ChefPaw*. https://www.chefpaw.com/blogs/news/homemade-dog-food

Tinnin, A. (2021, July 16). *Homemade dog food in the crockpot*. A Cup Full of Sass. https://www.acupfullofsass.com/homemade-dog-food-in-the-crockpot/

Tupler, T. (2011, August 4). *What's in a balanced dog food?* PetMD. https://www.petmd.com/dog/nutrition/evr_dg_whats_in_a_balanced_dog_food

Unleash the magic of your slow cooker. (n.d.). University of Arkansas System. https://www.uaex.uada.edu/counties/miller/Unleash%20the%20Magic%20of%20your%20Slow%20Cooker%206%20pages-%20Sept%202012.pdf

Williams, K. (n.d.). *My dog won't eat: Feeding picky eaters*. VCA Animal Hospital. https://vcahospitals.com/know-your-pet/feeding-canine-picky-eaters

IMAGE REFERENCES

Aceron, E. (2020). *Raw meat on white ceramic plate* [Image]. Unsplash. https://unsplash.com/photos/raw-meat-on-white-ceramic-plate-YlAmh_X_SsE

Bahara, V. (2020). *Stainless steel cooking pot on brown wooden chopping board* [Image]. Unsplash. https://unsplash.com/photos/stainless-steel-cooking-pot-on-brown-wooden-chopping-board-5FF8D5_0ls4

Briscoe, J. (2019). *Woman smiling while cooking* [Image]. Unsplash. https://unsplash.com/photos/woman-smiling-while-cooking-GrdJp16CPk8

Deachul, K. (2019). *Variety of cooked foods* [Image]. Unsplash. https://unsplash.com/photos/variety-of-cooked-foods-NOAzwcMzZJA

Ello. (2020). *Green and pink plastic container* [Image]. Unsplash. https://unsplash.com/photos/green-and-pink-plastic-container-AEU9UZstCfs

Goncharenok, M. (2020). *Person feeding a pet dog* [Image]. Pexels. https://www.pexels.com/photo/person-feeding-a-pet-dog-4422098/

Gruber, A. (2020). *Brown and white short coated dog on white and pink inflatable ring* [Image]. Unsplash. https://unsplash.com/photos/brown-and-white-short-coated-dog-on-white-and-pink-inflatable-ring-it3aC1K6sWQ

Hansel, L. (2020). *Pink and white oblong ornament* [Image]. Unsplash. https://unsplash.com/photos/pink-and-white-oblong-ornament-pKsgUVm6PC0

Hansel, L. (2020). *Sliced carrots* [Image]. Unsplash. https://unsplash.com/photos/sliced-carrots-QmtzIj7f5dc

Harijanto, Y. (2015). *Meat with sauce in black bowl* [Image]. Unsplash. https://unsplash.com/photos/meat-with-sauce-in-black-bowl-xKSRpUH0VZo

Keiwalinsarid, J. (2020). *Bowl of soup* [Image]. Pexels. https://www.pexels.com/photo/bowl-of-soup-3559899/

Khamseh, S. (2020). *Photo of lunch, food, meal, and label* [Image]. Unsplash. https://unsplash.com/photos/text-SRzVKw8l_tA

Lukas. (2018). *Sliced vegetables* [Image]. Pexels. https://www.pexels.com/photo/sliced-vegetables-952479/

McCudden, R. (2018). *Black and white dalmatian dog eating fruits* [Image]. Pexels. https://www.pexels.com/photo/black-and-white-dalmatian-dog-eating-fruits-770363/

Ryczek, H. (2023). *A whole chicken on a plate with a sprig of rosemary* [Image]. Unsplash. https://unsplash.com/photos/a-whole-chicken-on-a-plate-with-a-sprig-of-rosemary-pNcFMdEe09Q

Sebastian Coman Photography. (2019). *Grilled meat* [Image]. Unsplash. https://unsplash.com/photos/grilled-meat-1UanRBa1skQ

Shuraev, Y. (2021). *Woman sitting outside with her husky* [Image]. Pexels. https://www.pexels.com/photo/woman-sitting-outside-with-her-husky-9632393/

Vázquez, A. (2021). *Photo of grey, kitchen, measure, and measurement* [Image]. Unsplash. https://unsplash.com/photos/text-7iHhlSA2BRA

Winegeart, K. (2020). *Brown French bulldog in blue bucket* [Image]. Unsplash. https://unsplash.com/photos/brown-french-bulldog-in-blue-bucket-pQVecS8pBNY

Yousaf, U. (2020). *Sliced meat on brown wooden chopping board* [Image]. Unsplash. https://unsplash.com/photos/sliced-meat-on-brown-wooden-chopping-board-yizdlpAds9c

Made in United States
Troutdale, OR
07/29/2024

21634116R00051